From the host of the Expressive Espresso podcast

# SIP THIS HUSTLE

*The productivity guide for the full time employee who's also a side hustler*

## BY ALEXIS D'ANJOU-COLEY

EXPRESSIVE
ESPRESSO

Published by: Expressive Espresso Publishing LLC

www.alexis-danjou.com

Cover design by Alexis D'Anjou-Coley

Manufactured in the United States of America

ISBN: 978-0-578-60839-6

First Trade Paperback Edition: January 2020

# Dedication

To Jamarious, You're my number one with a lemonade. The hard worker, dedicated, and strong leader of our family. There are many things that I can say, which would be cliché. However, you already know how deep my love for you goes. Even when our water is tested against a hurricane, I'm reminded that this experience is something that I could not, would not, want to go through with anyone else. Thank you for loving me and our family unconditionally first.

To our kids, you all make me proud. May you continue to challenge us and help us grow in the process. May you continue to flourish into more than your potential and play your positions with intelligence, dignity, and grace. C6 is the base. C6 is the foundation. C6, no matter how blended it is, we will prevail. C6 forever and always.

To Mom, Ms. Perry, raising me within our small village and introducing me to the hustler mentality early on has benefited me in ways that I could never repay you for.

To Gdad, weekends in SoHo with you and Ma will always hold dear. Thank you for being the ultimate example of a black man.

To all the readers, listeners, and followers, thank you for allowing me to share my experiences with you as well as other entrepreneurs. This journey has been an experience that I'm enjoying and honored to be a part of. B1 always and sip this hustle daily

# Table of Contents

# Bell's palsy

[ˈbelz ˌpôlzē]
NOUN

• paralysis of the facial nerve causing muscular weakness in one side of the face.

At the age of nineteen, I dealt with a lot of

different challenges.  Two weeks prior we just welcomed the world to our daughter that was born in the winter but named after a different season. She was born a little less than seven pounds. As a new mom, the transition was very challenging. Not only was it challenging for us, I believe it was challenging for her as well. Autumn that is.

Fast forward to two weeks later I can remember, looking in the mirror, after taking a shower, newborn baby crying in the crib, thinking, what the f*** is wrong with my face? Taking it back to only a few days ago where I could go anywhere. Without having a sitter, without having anyone to answer to. And there I was looking at my newly right-sided slanted stroke face like what is going on??!! I wasn't completely aware of what was going on. All I knew was, I need to tell Autumn's father, I need to tell Ma, and I need to call the doctor. A few hours later, an emergency visit to my OB/GYN, then to the hospital I was diagnosed with Bell's palsy.

The doctor, by the way, had no sympathy. Maybe it was because of the stress of other patients. And having this young black mother who obviously didn't know what she was getting herself into wasn't really a priority.

At 33, I get it. I get the importance of prioritizing. At 19, I knew I would never be the same. Bell's palsy is something that I dealt with immediately after having my first child.

I didn't take any pictures at this time because the superficial aspect of me was there. At that time, I was given a discharge sheet of reasons why, and I even decided to make it a topic of my public speaking class presentation.

What you will not find googling the term is:

      a) College students can get this because of stress.
      b) There isn't really a cure for it because it only lasts
      about 2-3 weeks.
      c) Sleep deprivation can cause this.

Not only was I (we, everyone in the house) dealing with sleep deprivation, being a sophomore in college, having a new baby (new for me and my daughter's father), and dealing with the perception of people talking in the background.

Things like "you're never going to make it" "Didn't your daughter just have a baby at 19?" or "We can adopt your baby".

Hearing those things, although it hurt, I had to grow up and realize:

1.) There's a little person looking at me
2.) I need to focus on turning people's doubts into motivation.
3.) I must prove every doubter wrong.

Focus on the verb definition is to "pay particular attention to" As a side hustler, you want to pay attention to certain items, even as it pertains to your productivity.  Let's just be honest here.  Life will always get in the way.

Every side entrepreneur wants to be productive. It feels good to look at something tangible and say, "I created this. I made this. I did this."

To get things done. To check things off a list. To make a serious dent in your checklist.

Productivity looks different to different people, but the feeling is universal. For one person, creating an incredible presentation or meeting the needs of a specific client can make them feel amazing. For another, it may mean developing a new product or coming up with a new design.

For you, it may be completely different, but you know the good feeling you get by putting in a productive day.

**The learning curve:**

Life lessons always help us gain knowledge. Even going through the diagnosis of Bell's palsy, having a child out of wedlock, in college, and being young, all these events were major setbacks, like a hustler I ended up flipping all those negatives into a positive.
But of course, I had to have a plan. Setting a goal and achieving the goal is only one factor. Remaining focused during that goal and appreciating the journey is the learning curve.

How is this wife, mother, podcast host, side entrepreneur, and the full-time employee going to help you "sip this hustle"?

My motivators helped me.  The naysayers helped me.  But all in all, I had to plan and stay focused.

With the initial goal, once it's completed, it may need to be altered.  Think of it this way: There are more distractions now than ever before and in order to remain productive to that goal it takes focus.  Of course, you can receive a snippet of this on a social media post.  After reading this book I want you to challenge yourself.  Challenge yourself to remain productive during distractions.  Because with any goal, during the journey of reaching that goal, whether it is training for a 5k, become a DJ, or selling your own product, being productive during that time takes focus, ambition, and determination.

What will help you to remain productive while trying to reach a goal?  What happens after you've reached the goal?  It's in the sip this hustle lifestyle.

# Sip this hustle

[sip THis ˈhəsəl]

ADJECTIVE

• Achieving or producing a lifestyle goal in small doses.

VERB

• Starting the journey while having a full-time position to have a successful side hustle.

HASHTAG

• #sipthishustle

It's not just being busy on a day to day basis.  Look at my schedule:

## WEEKLY SCHEDULE

• * is every other weekend     • J = the youngest     • N = no     • Y = yes

| | M | T | W | T | F |
|---|---|---|---|---|---|
| Family | Y | Y | J | J | * Y |
| Work | Y | Y | Y | Y | Y |
| Cook | Y | Y | N | Y | N |
| Work Out | Y | Y | N | N | Y |
| Podcast | Y | Y | Y | Y | Y |
| Resume | Y | N | N | N | Y |
| Book | Y | Y | Y | Y | Y |

This schedule includes the goals that I want to accomplish throughout the week. Don't get me wrong, I'm not doing this by myself.  It takes a village for just one child, and the kids (including businesses) that my husband and I have, let's just say I think of them as more than a village.

They're the corporation of people who don't get the acknowledgment needed, but they all help with the agenda while maintaining what they have going on.

As an imperfect being, do I miss the mark of this schedule? Of course, I do!
It leaves me to miss what I'm doing the most (my podcast) to other aspects of my life that are a priority (family). Not to mention working overtime at an organization that I absolutely enjoy being a part of. With the different demands of projects, my weekends are spent ordering postmates, (even though we're on a tight budget).

Productivity encourages a true sense of purpose. It offers a deep feeling of accomplishment that's important to a happy and fulfilled life.

Being productive also gives you the freedom to spend more time with the ones you love and less time worrying about the things that are left unfinished.

If you're looking for that sense of purpose and happiness that can come from being productive, this book can help you focus on the things that will get you there.

Productivity isn't always easy. There are so many things that can cause your productivity to falter and even come to a complete stop.

As an entrepreneur, you're constantly battling a thousand distractions that can block creativity and derail a productive morning, afternoon, or evening. These distractions may stem from your personal life, or they may be work-related.

All-day long, you're receiving:

- Notifications
- Texts
- Instant messages
- Emails
- Social media pings
- Calls
- And a whole lot more!

Just as you start getting to important matters, your phone dings. It's a new message that you feel like you should probably check. You look at your phone and, the next thing you know, 45 minutes have passed. You've been sucked into the black hole of social media.

And even if you're able to set aside distractions, you may still feel like you're not really accomplishing anything.

You're busy… **but you're not productive.**

You're getting things done…

…**but you're not getting the right things done.**

You answer a lot of emails, reply to a lot of texts, and message a lot of people on Slack…

…**but still, come away each day feeling like you didn't accomplish what you wanted to.**

Have you ever felt like you were working hard, but getting nowhere? You go to bed exhausted, wake up exhausted, but you don't feel like you have anything to show for it. You know there must be a better way, but you just don't know where to start.

In this book, **you'll discover the 4 pillars of productivity.**

These four pillars will help you achieve a sense of accomplishment that you're really striving for. Instead of going to bed feeling defeated, with piles of work still sitting on the table, you can go to bed knowing that you've done enough for the day.

You've put in the work, and you can be fulfilled in what you've completed.

# Chapter 1

# Systems
# Over Goals

**"…I got my start by giving myself a start."**
**- Madam C.J. Walker. American Entrepreneur.**

You've probably been told that in order to be productive, you should set goals. Big goals. S.M.A.R.T. goals. Stretch goals.

The thinking goes that in order to achieve anything meaningful, you need to turn it into a goal.

Well… maybe.

While goals can be helpful, they aren't always ideal.

## The Problem with Goals

Goals have one big problem: **they have a termination point.**

In other words, you're not successful until you've reached your goal, and until you've reached the goal you might feel like:

- You're spinning your wheels, not going anywhere.
- You're a failure.
- You haven't achieved anything since the goal seems so distant.

Measuring success this way can make you feel defeated, especially if you have big, ambitious goals.

For example, if you want to own a Fortune 500 hundred company, nothing you do until you reach that goal will make you feel like you're succeeding. You may be making incredible strides in your business, but they will fall short compared to your hard-to-achieve goal.

Since goals have an "end", you never feel like a success until you've achieved your goal. And even when you achieve your goal, you simply must start all over again with the next goal.

And the reality is, you might not even know what the "next" goal should be. So, you feel aimless. You know you should be seeking to accomplish something, but you're not sure what that something should be.

Even worse, you might feel like since you already accomplished your goal you can go back to your old habits instead of pushing and growing. You lose all the forward progress that you made.

It's a setup to make you feel like a consistent failure.

# The Power of Systems

There is another, a better way!

They're called systems.

Systems allow you to:

- Make progress on your goals every single day
- Guarantee your success
- Help you reach your milestones
- Avoid the feeling that you're just spinning your wheels

## What are Systems?

Scott Adams, who you may know as the author of the famous Dilbert cartoons, wrote about systems in his book, How to Fail at Almost Everything and Still Win Big: Kind of the Story of My Life.

**He explained the difference between systems and goals like this:**

"Losing ten pounds may be a goal, while the system is learning to eat right."

Here's another example. Suppose your goal is to clean the house from top to bottom. You've spent the whole day cleaning, and you momentarily feel satisfied with what you've done.

However, if you have no system in place, your home will quickly go into disarray shortly thereafter.

**After a few days…**

…the dishes will overwhelm the sink, the laundry will pile up, and the floors will be a mess.

A system, on the other hand, would be a cleaning routine. Instead of cleaning the entire house in one day, you train yourself to do small tasks each day. The result is a house that's tidy for more than a few hours.

**Here's a business example:**

- **Goal:** Generate $50,000 in revenue over the next two months.

- **System:** Every morning you make three cold calls (or however many is necessary) to potential new customers.

The system ensures that you reach the end result.

Using a system doesn't mean that you have no goals. **It just means that you start to focus more on the process than the final destination.**

# So, What's Wrong with Goals?

You've probably been told your whole life to set lofty goals and work really hard to achieve them.

On its face, there's nothing wrong with having goals. Goals can inspire, motivate, and challenge us. They give us something to look forward to and a reason to continue striving.

**But goals can also be rigid and unmoving.**

Let's imagine you've set a firm goal for your company. You would like to make an X amount of sales by a certain date.

You really hustle to make those sales. You push your employees to do the same. You may make a lot of sales.

But what happens when you don t reach your goal amount?

Chances are…

…you'll feel like a failure.

All the sales that you *did* make won't bring you joy because you *didn't sell* enough. You'll feel unproductive and you may even want to quit.

What's unfortunate about this scenario is that you may have missed many opportunities along the way.

Bottom line?
**Being overly focused on a distant goal can easily give you tunnel vision.**

Your determination to complete a singular goal may have kept you from taking the time to develop a new product that could be sold for twice as much.

Scott Adams writes:

> "...if you focus on one particular goal, your odds of achieving it are better than if you have no goal. But you also miss out on opportunities that might have been far better than your goal...With a system, you are less likely to miss one opportunity because you were too focused on another. With a system, you are always scanning for any opportunity."

## Goals Limit Your Threshold for Happiness

The big issue with goals is that you're so narrowed in on a future time that you aren't happy until you hit that mark.

**Once you reach a goal:**

- The feeling of happiness will likely fade quickly.

- You'll then feel the need to achieve the next goal and the next.

- You're continually chasing something that is, at its best, fleeting.

Productivity expert James Clear has also written extensively about systems versus goals.

**In his book, Atomic Habits, he explains:**

"When you fall in love with the process rather than the product, you don't have to wait to give yourself permission to be happy. You can be satisfied anytime your system is running. And a system can be successful in many different forms, not just the one you first envision."

## What Happens When You Reach Your Goal?

You may also realize that once you've achieved a certain goal, you have nothing else to work towards.

For example, let's suppose you set a personal goal to run a marathon.

**In order to achieve your goal:**

- You forced yourself to go to the gym four times a week.
- You went running even though you didn't feel like it.
- You cut things out of your diet even though you didn't want to.

You worked hard, but you didn't enjoy the process that got you there.

Once you met your goal, you couldn't stand the thought of going back to that regimented schedule.

Pretty soon, you've abandoned your running routine and you've gone back to your former lifestyle. Your muscles soften, you put the weight back on, and you can't stand to look at your running shoes.

What went wrong?

**You were focused on the goal, but the system was unbearable.**

You probably started training for a marathon because you wanted to be healthier and stronger.

Scott Adams explains that while you can set a goal to exercise three to four times a week on a rigid schedule if you're not enjoying the exercise, there's a much higher risk that you're going to give it up.

You may do it for a time, but in the long run, you'll probably lack the willpower to continue because it feels like a punishment.

Instead, he suggests choosing to be active each day to a level that feels good.
**In this scenario...**

- You're training yourself that being active is positive.

- You're going to get a psychological lift from the exercise.

- You're slowly training your body and mind to enjoy being active as opposed to hating it.

You'll naturally want to challenge yourself as you continue to enjoy being more active. Your original activity level may start with short, slow walks, but you may eventually find that you like running as well.

**You'll do so because you want to, and not because you're forcing yourself to.**

# How Do Systems Help Side Hustlers?

First and foremost, systems are much more flexible than goals.
If you have a type-A personality, this shift may make you feel a little uncomfortable at first. It may feel like you're giving up control by not focusing so much energy on a future outcome.

The big question you have to ask yourself is: **What happens when you shift your focus from a concrete goal to the process that gets you there?**

If you're focused on the system, does that mean you're abandoning your goals and wandering aimlessly?

The short answer is: no. Here's why.

Suppose a sports coach chooses to focus on picking great players, developing incredible plays, and creating effective practice routines instead of winning.

What would be the result? They'l probably have a winning team.

James Clear writes:

> "Every Olympian wants to win a gold medal. Every candidate wants to get the job. And if successful and unsuccessful people share the same goals, then the goal cannot be what differentiates the winners from the losers...The goal had always been there. It was only when they implemented a system of continuous small improvements that they achieved a different outcome."

**In order for your business to be successful, it's vital to understand what is working and what isn't working in your *process.***

Think about the things in your system that are working and the things that are not.

**What does your hiring process look like?**

- Do you have strong employees that fit your vision?

- If not, what practices can you change to hire better employees?

**Think about your marketing campaign and the system that drives it.**

- Is it working?

- What changes can you implement in your system to reach more customers and drive more business?

**Now think about your products or services and the systems you have in place to support them.**

- What can you do to improve your product?

- How can you streamline the process and make things more efficient?

- Are your products or services testing well?

- If not, what can you do to improve them?

These small, day-to-day improvements will make you feel successful, fulfilled, and productive. Learning how to push through daily struggles will bring you confidence and happiness in a way that's hard to reach goals never will.

A system teaches you how to become better at what you do, and it significantly develops your skill level. If something isn't working well, you have the flexibility to change it and move on.

You still have the skills that you developed, but you can now use them in a new direction.

That's the gift of a system.

# #STH Chapter One Recap:

- Plan the goal
- Enjoy the process: What's working? What isn't working? Adjust accordingly and while you're doing so, enjoy the process.
- Revisit the process after the goal is completed and address what needs to be adjusted.

# Chapter 2

# The Early Bird Gets Everything Done

"…the morning came, the night leaves.  A little of a workaholic, sh*t I might be.  Up at 6 in the morning like I'm Ice T.  Spent a grip on the Malcolm X, Spike Lee."
- **Nipsey Hussle.  Rapper, entrepreneur, and community activist.**
  **Late Nights and Early Mornings**

There's nothing quite like the peaceful calm of the early morning hours. And the fact is, **rising early is one of the key things that most successful entrepreneurs do.**

The early morning hours are one of the best times to tackle the most important tasks. Rising early allows you to accomplish great things before most of the world has even woken up.

This "mind over mattress" thinking has been around for a long time.

You may even be familiar with Benjamin Franklin's quote, "Early to bed and early to rise, makes a man healthy, wealthy, and wise."

**There are numerous successful entrepreneurs who are early risers:**

> • Apple CEO Tim Cook gets up as early as 3:45 am.

> • Michelle Gas, CEO of Kohl's department stores, gets up at 4:30 am to go running.

> • Former PepsiCo CEO Indra Nooyi rises at 4:00 am and is in the office by 7:00. In 2012, she told

Fortune, "They say sleep is a gift that God gives you...That's one gift I was never given."

● Twitter co-founder, Jack Dorsey, wakes up at 5:30 am to meditate and go for a six-mile jog.

● Starbucks CEO, Howard Schultz, is up at 4:00 am and in the office by 6:00 am.

● Richard Branson, a business entrepreneur behind the Virgin group of companies, rises at 5:45 am for an early morning workout and breakfast.

There are more examples of these early bird business machines.

What makes early risers successful, and how do you become an early riser?

# What Does the Science Say?

You may be wondering if this old adage is actually true. Do early risers really live happier more productive lives?

Here's what the researchers have to say about it.

# Night Owls are More Prone to Negative Thought Patterns

In 2014, the Department of Psychology at Binghamton University completed a study that included 100 undergraduate students. Their study found that both people who get less sleep, and those who delay sleep, are prone to Repetitive Negative Thinking (RNT).

RNT is a transdiagnostic disorder that can be observed in other disorders such as depression and anxiety. It's correlated with high levels of worry and negative thought patterns.

# Early Risers Increase Their Chance of Success

In 2010, Harvard Business Review released a study by biologist Christoph Randler about early risers.

367 university students participated in his survey, and they were asked what times of the day they were most energetic. They were also asked how willing and able they were to take action or change a situation to their advantage.

Randler reported, "A higher percentage of the morning people agreed with statements that indicate proactivity, such as 'I spend time identifying long-range goals for myself' and 'I feel in charge of making things happen.'"

He went on to say:

> "My earlier research showed that they tend to get better grades in school, which get them into better colleges, which then leads to better job opportunities. Morning people also anticipate problems and try to minimize them, my survey showed. They're proactive. A number of studies have linked this trait, proactivity, with better job performance, greater career success, and higher wages."

A similar study was conducted in 2008 by Kendry Clay at the University of North Texas. The study focused on 824 undergraduate students who were enrolled in psychology classes at the university. They were asked questions about their sleep habits and daytime functioning.

The study found that students who preferred the morning had higher GPAs, and those who preferred the evening had lower GPAs.

Both studies had the same conclusion: **Early risers have a higher chance of success.**

# 7 Ways to be an Early Riser

Rising early might sound like a good plan, but it's not always as easy as it sounds.

Thankfully, there are many things you can do to jump-start the day and ditch the bed.

Things to keep in mind while setting up your morning routine:

1) What is the first thing you want to do each morning?

2) What is the second thing you want to do each morning?

3) What will make your morning feel like a success?

4) What is the most important daily task you'll do each morning?

5) What do you consider "success?" Do you want to accumulate a fortune? Accolades? Community?

## Tip #1: Go to Bed Earlier

One of the easiest ways to get out of bed in the morning is to go to bed earlier at night.

The late evening hours might feel like a good time to be productive, but the **truth is:**

- You have a limited threshold for productivity.

- Your progress is going to stall.
- Your work is probably going to get sloppy.

Instead, do your most productive work during the daytime hours and leave the evening for rest and time with family and friends.

Some people are more prone to staying up late and sleeping in late, but this sleep pattern can be modified. Try going to bed one hour earlier and getting up one hour earlier to start.

## Tip #2: Turn off the Screens

We live in a world full of screens - smartphones, tablets, computers, and televisions. We're surrounded by screens.

While these tools can be extremely helpful for business, they can also affect your sleep.

**The National Sleep Foundation says that technology/screens can affect our sleep in three very big ways:**

1. **They suppress melatonin**, the hormone that controls your sleep/wake cycle.

2. **They keep your brain active.** By keeping your mind engaged with television or work, you're telling your brain that it's time to stay awake.

3. **Your alerts can wake you up at night**. If you keep your mobile phone next to your bed, the sounds of emails, texts, and notifications can disturb your sleep.

To prevent technology from disturbing your precious sleep, turn it off or put it away a few hours before you go to bed. This will help your mind unwind and get you ready for sleep.

While many people use their phone for an alarm clock, this creates a huge temptation to check social media or try to fit in a few more minutes of work late at night. Do yourself a favor and go buy an alarm clock. Charge your cell phone in another room and get rid of the nighttime distractions.

## Tip #3: Create a Sleep Routine

Creating a sleep routine is what pediatricians recommend to parents that desperately want their babies and toddlers to go to bed at night.

However, this idea is not limited to children. **A sleep routine is an outstanding way for anyone to get the sleep they need.**

If possible, pick the same time to go to bed and to rise every day. Your body will adjust to this schedule and you may find that, eventually, you won't even need an alarm clock to wake up.

**The National Sleep Foundation suggests:**

- Finding a relaxing routine activity away from bright lights

- Trying to avoid activities that can cause excitement or stress

If you need something to occupy your thoughts before bed, try reading a book instead of watching a movie. Reading is known for reducing stress and helping you get a good night's sleep. According to a study conducted by Cognitive Neuropsychologist Dr. David Lewis, reading can reduce stress by 68%.

**Other things you can include in your nighttime routine are:**

- A warm, non-caffeinated drink
- Meditation or prayer
- A warm bath
- Breathing routines
- Using an app like "Calm", which helps you wind down each night

## Tip #4: Get Some Exercise

Getting a good night's rest can be as easy as putting in some good exercise during the day. Intense exercise is the most conducive for a good night's rest, but any level of activity is helpful.

Exercise has been found to increase time spent in deep sleep, improve the quality of sleep, and it can help you sleep longer.

In addition, physical activity is known to reduce stress and anxiety -- two things that can greatly affect someone's ability to fall asleep and stay asleep.

## Tip #5: Keep Your Alarm Clock at a Distance

If your number one difficulty is simply waking up in the morning, set your alarm clock out of reach. If you can't keep your hands off the snooze button, this will force you to get out of bed. Once you're up, ensure you don't crawl back into the covers.

## Tip #6: A Splash of Cold Water

If you're extra groggy in the AM, you can always try splashing cold water in your face. This cold water will help energize you and snap you into awake mode.

## Tip #7: Give Yourself a Reason to Get Up

**Thinking of a compelling reason to get out of bed in the morning may be your strongest motivator for early rising.**

Your reason for getting up in the morning may vary from someone else's but give yourself a good reason to wake up. Choose something that will be effective day after day.

Knowing that you can be more productive early in the morning may be enough to get out of your warm blankets. If not, maybe the thought of a tasty breakfast or a hot cup of coffee might be your reason for leaving your cozy covers.

## #STH Chapter Two recap:

- Early mornings versus late nights are more beneficial.
- Understand your "why" to remain focused. Repeat that mantra. It needs to motivate you enough to get up.
- Reference the 7 ways to become an early riser.

# Chapter 3

# Kill Your Distractions

**"…it isn't the mountains ahead to climb that wear you out; it's the pebble in your shoe."
- Muhammad Ali. Heavyweight champion boxer and greatest sports figure.**

You know the feeling. You've prepped yourself to buckle down and start crossing things off your to-do list. It's a mile long, and it just keeps growing. You're finally in the right mindset and you're ready to fly.

You're completely geared up to knock out your list, and you're 100% ready for that feeling of relief and satisfaction you'll have at the end of a full productive day.

Then the phone buzzes -- it's a text message.

Your laptop dings with a new email.

Your phone lights up with a new instant message.

An employee walks into your office with an important question.

Your phone rings – it's a non-work-related call.

You need a cup of coffee. You must use the bathroom. You're starting to get hungry.

Before you know it, the whole morning is blown, and you don't have anything to show for it.

Unfortunately, **distractions are one of the main killers of productivity.** You have a lot of things coming at you, and many of them are keeping you from focusing on what truly matters.

While you're busy with these distractions, you're not actually accomplishing anything.

So how can you eliminate these distractions and get to the most important stuff?

**5 Tips to get rid of distractions**

1. Make plans the night before
2. Cut out social media
3. Create boundaries
4. Create a productive space
5. Don't make it all about WORK

**Here are 5 tips to get rid of the distractions and get back on track.**

## Tip #1: Make Plans the Night Before

Making plans the day before can be a helpful trick to help you stay focused on the following day.

You don't have to plan out every decision but make choices about simple things that might be distractions during the day.

**For example:**

- What you'll wear for the day
- What lunch you'll eat
- The way you'll get to work

When you're tired in the morning, these decisions are probably going to be harder to make and can easily occupy your thought processes.

You can also set a rough schedule for yourself. For example, you may decide that you won't check your e-mail or answer text messages until you've completed two important tasks. From 8 a.m. to 10 a.m. you'll focus solely on a specific project.

# Tip #2: Cut Out Social Media

It's now estimated that people are spending 2 hours and 22 minutes a day on social media. That's a great stat if you're trying to reach customers, but a terrible one for productivity.

Yes, social media can be a necessary resource for marketing and sales, but...

- Constantly checking your personal notifications
- Taking the time to respond to various rants
- Endlessly scrolling through pictures on Instagram

...Isn't going to help your business.

Social media is a black hole and a major time suck. Notifications and social media, in general, can be incredibly addictive.

**Here are some strategies to help you manage your social media time:**

- Set a schedule for when you'll go on social media – for example, between 10 - 11 a.m. and 4 - 5 p.m.

- Use built-in tools like "iOS Screen Time" and "Android Digital Wellbeing" to monitor or restrict social media use on your phone.

- Turn off all non-business-related notifications so you're not feeling the constant pull of "dings" distracting you.

Use your business social media accounts to engage with real customers, tweet about your newest products, and post beautiful pictures. After that, put your phone away and focus on your other tasks.

## Tip #3: Create Boundaries

In any given workday you'll have to field important calls. There may be some lines of communication that are necessary to your workday, but there are others that can be set aside.

Give yourself periods during your day when you don't check your phone, emails, or Slack messages.

Some side hustlers choose the early morning to return emails and engage with customers on social media. Others choose to focus on their list of tasks before creating new tasks introduced by outside messages.

**Choose the rhythm that works best for you** but ensure that you stick to it. It's vitally important to set times of the day when you're not in constant contact with outside interruptions.

If possible, it's also a good plan to leave at least one day a week when you're not scheduled for a meeting. This can give you a free day to complete tasks and stay productive.

# Tip #4: Create a Productive Space

If you're working at home or in an office, it's important to create a space where you can feel productive.

**Remember the 3Ps:**
**Productivity produces productivity.**

In other words, if you were productive in a particular space, your brain will want to be productive there again. You'll associate that place with the good feeling that you had the last time you were able to crush it at work.

Likewise, if you have a certain space that you associate with entertainment -- perhaps the living room where the TV is -- you'll want to do those fun things when you're there.

**Keep your fun places and your workplaces separate and make your workspace conducive for work.**

If you want your workplace to promote work, keep it tidy. A cluttered or messy space will distract you. Even if you don't feel like you have to clean it up, the disorganization will keep you from getting to your tasks.

Keep your workplace simple and easy to maintain and ensure that it has a door so you can shut out distractions when necessary.

Sometimes when I have a tight deadline with my full-time position, I need to go to a quiet space. A conference room that isn't being used at that time, or a loft.

# Tip #5: It Can't All Be Work

While there are a few successful individuals who are truly all work and no play, most human beings aren't geared that way. In fact, we're not really meant to be.

Psychiatrist Stuart Brown, the founder of the National Play Institute, understands the importance of taking time to play.

In his book Play: How It Shapes the Brain, Opens the Imagination, and Invigorates the Soul, he writes, "The truth is that play seems to be one of the most advanced methods nature has invented to allow a complex brain to create itself."

Play opens up a person for creativity and relieves us of our heavy workloads. Some workplaces like Google have even built-in areas at work for play. These spaces are meant to foster creativity and relieve stress in the workplace.

Dr. Brown also explains in his book:

"...there is a kind of magic in play. What might seem like a frivolous or even childish pursuit is ultimately beneficial. It's paradoxical that a little bit of "nonproductive" activity can make one enormously more productive and invigorated in other aspects of life."

Most human beings grow frustrated and unproductive when they force themselves to work constantly and enjoy very little. This is a system that is ultimately unsustainable.

**There are several things that a side entrepreneur can do to combat this:**

1. **Make work enjoyable.** Find ways to make the things you do at work pleasurable and exciting as opposed to drudgery work.

2. **Plan to have breaks during the day.** Walk around the building, eat a good lunch, or take a coffee break.

    • It may seem like these things are distractions on their own, but when coupled with more intense sessions of work, they are simply something to work forward to.

3. **Choose a quitting time.** Choose a part of the day to set aside work and be finished. It's extremely important to have time set aside in the day to give attention to friends and family.

- It's also important to enjoy relaxation, play, and leisure. This gives you time to bounce back from the workday and start fresh the next day.

4. **Take a vacation**. Plan for certain times of the year to be non-work times. Enjoy your relationships with others and find ways to have fun. Set aside the phones, emails, and messages and focus on the other things in life that matter to you.

You may never be able to cut out all distractions built-in but limiting them can greatly enhance your chances of success. Reduce social media, limit communication, and make time for play, and you'll soon see that your productive periods are a lot more successful.

## #STH Chapter Three recap:

- Kill your distractions by perfecting your planning techniques.
- Get back on track from your distractions using the 5 tips.
- Implement these practices to help you get back on track.

# Chapter 4

# Slay Your Dragons

**"…slay trick, or you get eliminated, I slay."**
**- Beyoncé Knowles-Carter.**
**Actress, musician, and entrepreneur.**
**Formation**

The final pillar we will focus on is prioritizing your workday. While it's easy to start the day with low hanging fruit, like email, the most productive side hustlers focus on getting their most important task done first.

**Experts always recommend that you slay your dragon (hardest task) first.**

Mark Twain said, "If it's your job to eat a frog, it's best to do it first thing in the morning. And if it's your job to eat two frogs, it's best to eat the biggest one first."

In other words, tackle the hardest things before you do anything else.

## What Does the Research Say?

How does this theory stack up in real life? Does it really make sense to do the hard things first?

In 2017, Harvard Business School released a working paper called Task Selection and Workload: A Focus on Completing Easy Tasks Hurts Long-Term Performance.

The study discussed in the working paper was conducted in an emergency department in a metropolitan hospital. They…" assembled [their] data from the emergency department for twenty-four months in fiscal years 2006-2007 involving over 90,000 distinct patient encounters."

The study was meant to discover how starting with easier tasks versus harder tasks might affect productivity.

*The study concluded that completing easier tasks does create a short-term sense of satisfaction, but it can negatively impact long-term productivity.*

The paper explains:

> "By selecting the easier task (exploitation) an individual gets work done quicker – and likely feels good doing it. However, by choosing the harder task (exploration) one creates an opportunity to learn. Although always selecting the harder task may be suboptimal, if one continually chooses the exploitation path then longer-term performance suffers."

In other words, a short-term victory feels good at the moment. It makes a person feel productive when they accomplish something.

However, because they are not pushing themselves to learn and overcome the harder tasks, they're limiting their potential.

Not only that, but the study found that the physicians who habitually chose the easier tasks first were less profitable to the hospital in the long run.

# Put That Plan into Action

Only you know what your most difficult or complicated tasks are but do your best to take on those jobs first. Hit them first thing in the morning when you're at your strongest. Even if your difficult tasks don't take you the longest, they're going to take a lot more effort.

As the day goes on, your ability to focus diminishes. Your willpower may fall apart, and you'll want to avoid your work and put it off until the next day.

If you choose your hardest jobs first, you'll be able to finish the day up with your easiest work. That feeling of productivity from easy tasks will help propel you into the next day when you're ready to slay your dragons once again.

# #STH Chapter Four recap:

- Plan the goal
- Enjoy the process: What's working?  What isn't working?  Adjust accordingly and while you're doing so, enjoy the process.
- Revisit the process after the goal is completed and address what needs to be adjusted.

# Chapter 5

# Fresh fruit

**"…knowledge is knowing a tomato is a fruit;
wisdom is not putting it in a fruit salad."
- Miles Kington. British journalist,
musician, and broadcaster.**

The fresh fruit of productivity is well within your grasp. You want that good feeling of productivity and it's entirely in your control.

The four pillars included in this book are actionable ideas that you can start today:

- **Pillar #1.** Develop a system that works for you. Make it sustainable and continue tweaking it for the best results.

- **Pillar #2.** Wake up early in the morning, ready for the day while the rest of the world sleeps.

- **Pillar #3.** Cut out the countless distractions that prohibit your work instead of enhancing it.

- **Pillar #4.** Overcome your most difficult tasks first. Afterward, enjoy the fruits of your labor with an easier afternoon or evening.

Your new and productive workstyle will help you live that happy and fulfilled life that so many people are seeking.

At the end of the day, you can put your work aside and invest in the relationships in your life that are most meaningful. You can rest easy knowing that you gave your best effort and put in a productive and fruitful workday.

## Outro

# Sip This Hustle

**"...until we meet again, have a great week."**
**- Alexis D'Anjou-Coley. Podcast host of**
**Expressive Espresso, side serial entrepreneur,**
**and full-time employee.**

**T**he roadblocks of having Bell's palsy didn't deter me from the main goal. It was the journey in between that I can honestly look back and appreciate the obstacles that could've played over in my mind and left me stuck. I'm sure you know a few people with that mentality. This book is not for them though, it's for you. You know those late nights and early mornings. You know those struggles with finances piling up or working with an unmotivated client that you may have to fire.

Initially with Expressive Espresso the podcast, my goal was to inspire those like me. After a few years into the podcast, that goal has pivoted into inspiring those who are side entrepreneurs now and enjoy their jobs too. The goal may pivot again. However, the premise remains the same. Inspiring side hustlers with the good, the bad, and unfortunate.

Let's focus on our time management to remain productive. In addition to the four pillars used in the book. Pay attention to your time. Which is essential for side hustlers.

There are 1,440 minutes in each day. Most people are awake for about 16 hours out of the day. That means you have about 960 minutes to do what you need to do in order to have a successful day. This may seem daunting and it may seem inspiring. Regardless, it's important to be cognizant of the ways you spend your time.

On average, humans are able to focus for about 20 minutes at a time. However, it's possible to be focused for 20 minutes and then repeatedly refocus.

You can use this information to your advantage when you estimate how long each task will take. If something will take 4 hours, look at it in 20-minute sections. How much of this project can you get done in 20 minutes? How much can you get done in one hour?

**Take Planned Breaks**

**Maintain your attention on each task but be sure to take a break every 90 minutes.** If 90 minutes seems too long, you can also take breaks every 50 minutes. 15 to 20 minutes is a perfect length of time to give your brain a refreshing break.

You can practice being mindful of your time by being mindful during your timed breaks. Practicing a quick mindfulness activity is more effective than taking a break to get on social media or read the news.

**Mindfulness enables you to calm your mind and come to the present moment.** Social media stimulates the mind and distracts from the present moment.

Try these activities during work breaks:

> **Meditate.** You can meditate for just a few minutes. Sit up straight in your chair. Close your eyes or focus on one point ahead of you. Start to simply pay attention to your breath. Notice, "I am inhaling, I am exhaling."

**Go on a walk.** Embrace the feeling of fresh air and sunshine by taking a step away from your work and going on a walk. Leave your phone behind. Simply observe and notice the greenery, the sound of the cars, and the color of the sky.

**Take a coloring break.** Grab a coloring break and set a timer for ten minutes. Use those minutes to relax and color. This exercise will help keep your mind engaged without thinking about other things.

**Notice your five senses.** Take a moment to notice all of your senses. What do you hear, see, smell, taste, and feel? Go through all of your muscle groups and relax them, starting with your toes and ending with your ears.

## Set Reminders: Check Yourself

Set reminders for yourself to help notify you of an upcoming transition in your day. These small alerts can serve as a line of accountability when you're trying to practice new habits.

If you notice a "ding" five minutes before it's time to move on to your next task, you'll be able to find a stopping point and make a smooth transition to the next item of business.

**You can also take advantage of the opportunity that an alert presents.**

Use a small moment in your transition to acknowledge your day and check that your focus is on the task at hand. You don't always have to stop what you're doing in order to be mindful. You can take advantage of moments at work where you can bring your attention to exactly what you're doing.

If your next task calls for movement, bring your focus to your walking. Feel the ground beneath your shoes and focus on your breath, even if just for a moment.

It's easy to look to the future and concern ourselves with imagined scenarios that we truly cannot predict. **These small moments of mindfulness can provide a chance to let go of worry and focus on the task at hand without disrupting your day.**

How Does Mindfulness Affect Productivity?

An ability to focus on the present moment brings about a stronger connection to the task at hand rather than your entire to-do list. Those who practice mindfulness are less affected by distractions.

**Mindfulness increases productivity by creating a manageable stream of thoughts that do not overwhelm.** By practicing mindfulness regularly, you're likely to increase your ability to regulate emotions. This stability provides focus on only the thoughts that count.

Treat your time with care and attention. The best way to be mindful of your time is to be aware and conscious of what you do and when you do it. You can do this by creating a system, or a routine, for each day.

By sharing my mistakes and other side hustler's mistakes, you can sip this hustle and determine your own.

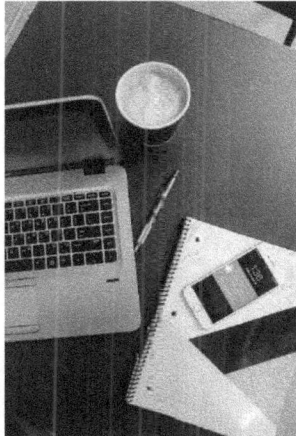

# MY MONTHLY PLANNER

## JANUARY

**To-Do List**

**My Goals This Month**

**Notes/Ideas**

# MY MONTHLY PLANNER

## FEBRUARY

**To-Do List**

**My Goals This Month**

**Notes/Ideas**

# MY MONTHLY PLANNER

## MARCH

**To-Do List**

**My Goals This Month**

**Notes/Ideas**

# MY MONTHLY PLANNER

### APRIL

**To-Do List**

**My Goals This Month**

**Notes/Ideas**

# MY MONTHLY PLANNER

## MAY

**To-Do List**

**My Goals This Month**

**Notes/Ideas**

# MY MONTHLY PLANNER

## JUNE

**To-Do List**

**My Goals This Month**

**Notes/Ideas**

# MY MONTHLY PLANNER

## JULY

**To-Do List**

**My Goals This Month**

**Notes/Ideas**

# MY MONTHLY PLANNER

## AUGUST

**To-Do List**

**My Goals This Month**

**Notes/Ideas**

# MY MONTHLY PLANNER

## SEPTEMBER

**To-Do List**

**My Goals This Month**

**Notes/Ideas**

# MY MONTHLY PLANNER

**OCTOBER**

**To-Do List**

**My Goals This Month**

**Notes/Ideas**

# MY MONTHLY PLANNER

## NOVEMBER

**To-Do List**

**My Goals This Month**

**Notes/Ideas**

# MY MONTHLY PLANNER

## DECEMBER

**To-Do List**

**My Goals This Month**

**Notes/Ideas**

SIP THIS HUSTLE NOTES:

SIP THIS HUSTLE NOTES:

SIP THIS HUSTLE NOTES:

SIP THIS HUSTLE NOTES:

SIP THIS HUSTLE NOTES:

*Scan me*

**To hear the latest episode of
Expressive Espresso**

**CREATE YOUR SIDE
HUSTLE OVER THE
WEEKEND**

**THE NEW E-COURSE**

**APRIL 2020**

# ALEXIS D'ANJOU-COLEY

Podcast host, consulting, and beyond

alexis-danjou.com

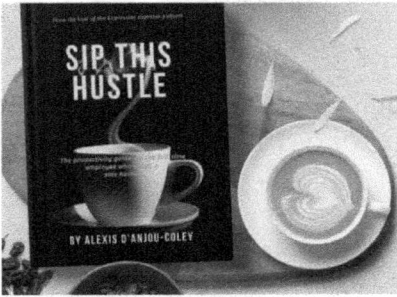

## CONNECT WITH US

**Podcast**
itunes | spotify | iheartradio | podomatic

**Email Address**
eethepodcast@gmail.com

**Phone Number**
(336) 365 8464